VIRGINIA

Photographs by David Alan Harvey
Text by James S. Wamsley

GRAPHIC ARTS CENTER PUBLISHING COMPANY
PORTLAND, OREGON

Graphic Arts Center Publishing Company, Portland, Oregon
International Standard Book Number 0-912856-66-1
Library of Congress Catalog Card Number 80-85368
Copyright© 1981 by Graphic Arts Center Publishing Company
P.O. Box 10306, Portland, Oregon 97210 • 503/224-7777
Typesetting • Paul O. Giesey/Adcrafters
Printer • Graphic Arts Center
Bindery • Lincoln & Allen
Printed in the United States of America

We wish to thank the National Geographic Society for allowing
us to reprint two photographs taken by David Alan Harvey.
Page 5 appeared in "Tangier Island", *National Geographic Magazine*,
p. 705, November, 1973; page 18 appeared in "Virginia",
National Geographic Magazine, pp.616-617, November, 1974.
Both are used here by permission of the publisher.

Page ii: Migrating geese spangle the sunset at Back Bay National
Wildlife Refuge, south of Virginia Beach. *Page 5:* Tidewater
moonlight softens the prim lines of a house on Chesapeake Bay, the
vast inland sea at Virginia's doorstep.

One family, nine generations: ownership of Shirley Plantation dates to the middle 1600s, although the present house was built around 1740. *Left:* Poplar-lined drive at Shirley beckons the visitor to an unchanged past. *Overleaf:* Fall comes first to Highland County, where Virginia's highest mean altitude assures a non-Dixie climate.

The Potomac River, supreme in drama, plunges through Great Falls, near Washington. *Right:* Early snow, Nelson County. *Overleaf:* Clouds or fog? It's all the same in the ridge-rimmed Shenandoah Valley near Front Royal, where blue nimbi greet the spring. Near here were the valley's first settlements.

Country music festivals are for the young and old, as impromptu jam sessions link generations and harmonies. *Right:* Market time calls forth the golden weed from tobacco curing barns. This crop is bound for Danville, where bright leaf is considered king. *Overleaf:* The Governor's Palace at Colonial Williamsburg mirrors two-centuries-old days of British pomp and power.

VIRGINIA

In my earliest memory the Model T Ford was a faintly ridiculous artifact from another age, but still it abounded in the Virginia countryside. Model T s would roll past our house trailing noises that ranged (depending on bearing wear and piston slap) from a friendly chuckle to the roar of a threshing machine. Most were three-door tourings. Their tops and side curtains snapped and fluttered tightly, like black, dusty sails.

Our house stood on the northwest edge of Staunton, and the street thus defaced by unfashionable Model T s was the beginning of a historic road called the Parkersburg Pike. Staunton was the trading center for northwest Virginia. Saturdays, the flivver traffic was heavy. Farm families came from as far as the West Virginia border to shop at Worthington's Hardware and Leggett's Dry Goods.

In those Depression days, Virginia's country people *looked* like country people. The men dressed in bib overalls, with dress shirts buttoned at the neck, without ties. The women wore flowered frocks. Late Saturday, their owners' shopping done, the Model T s clattered westward out of town, bags of feed and fertilizer lashed to their fenders.

Quaint as the scene may strike you, its memory is insufficient to certify me, aged precisely half a century, as a vestige of Currier and Ives' America. For that I must remember the drovers.

Delivering animals on foot was fairly rare even in the 1930s, and it made a vivid impression on a boy of around five. The herd would undulate down our road like a hairy avalanche in slow motion, framed in a cloud — an aura — of dust. There was a wonderful racket of bellowing cattle, or nasal sheep, and sometimes — unless memory betrays me — both. The drovers strode along, hot and filthy, with sturdy sticks. There was always at least one young boy, in bib overalls and no shirt, a scrawny little runt, who scampered beside the herd. I envied his glorious, dirty freedom.

We had close ties in the mountain country, the dark and rumpled Alleghenies, which were home to Model T s and drovers. Some Sundays we'd drive out in the 1931 Buick, past crumbling stagecoach inns named Buckhorn Tavern, West Augusta, and Mountain House. We drove through foothill notches screened by hemlocks, and across North Mountain and Shenandoah Mountain and Shaw's Ridge. In the small valley of the Cowpasture River we visited an ancient aunt, whose spare white farmhouse smelled of generations of burning locust logs, dried apples, and salty Virginia ham. She lived at the foot of Bullpasture Mountain, along whose rocky peaks Stonewall Jackson had punished General Milroy with a certain grim relish in the opening battle of Jackson's Valley Campaign. "God blessed our arms with victory at McDowell," Jackson wired Lee. It was an Old Testament observation worthy of both Jackson and the rocky, gaunt, Gothic fastness of Highland County.

Highland. Every man needs a dream place, and for others of my circle it was often an island, with a name like the mutter of surf or the rustle of papaya leaves, but that was not for me. Shangri-La was in the mountains, remember? There was never a doubt where mine was. Not east, across the pastel airiness of the Blue Ridge, but west, with the Saturday Fords and the drovers and Aunt Minnie.

I didn't know it, but already I was marked by a common Virginia whimsicality: a sense of place, a strong identification with the state plus a sense of belonging in a still tighter-focused locale. Perhaps, because Virginians prefer restraint to extravagant talk about the beauties and history of their state, they are not perceived by outsiders as harboring fierce devotion to their common home. But with time and tragedy in the background, Virginians feel the history of their tribe. That is why Lee cast his lot with the Confederacy, though he suspected the war was lost before it began. He didn't care that much about a nascent Southern nation; he detested slavery, and he was a patriotic believer in the Federal Republic. But when decision time came, he reacted like the tribal chief that he was. He would defend the common home.

Lee's biographer, Dr. Douglas Southall Freeman, said Virginians practice a form of mild Shintoism, an ancient religion involving reverence for ancestors, the practice of rituals, and the maintenance of shrines. People from many other states simply don't feel that way. But coming to Virginia, a lot of them become enthusiastic converts and the most ardent historic preservationists.

None of that was known to me, growing up in Staunton during the Depression. One of my favorite pastimes was playing next door in Mr. Charley Bryan's stable. Mr. Bryan had been gassed in World War I action in France and somehow had succeeded in bringing back an ancient Fiat taxi, with an open chauffeur's compartment linked by speaking tube to the luxurious passenger's tonneau. Resting on a bed of straw in the dim stable, the old car was pure magic. Years after World War II, when the Fiat was dragged out and sacrificed in a scrap drive, I heard it was one of the legendary Taxis of the Marne.

When I wasn't in the Fiat, I was often over in Gypsy Hill Park, admiring Woodrow Wilson's Pierce-Arrow in the Billy Sunday Tabernacle. Sunday, an evangelist when Model T s were new, with an implacably low-brow style achieved a national success that included the erection of tabernacles to accommodate his extensive tours. Mercifully for the ecclesiastical peace of sedately-churched Staunton, Mr. Sunday had just been summoned to that great sawdust trail in the sky, and his tabernacle had been sequestered by the city for miscellaneous shelter.

At that time, the memory of Woodrow Wilson had not jelled into hagiolatry. Dead only fifteen years or so, he was out of place with the seven other Virginia-born presidents — George Washington, Thomas Jefferson, James Madison, James Monroe, William Henry Harrison, John Tyler, and Zachary Taylor — who were long-embalmed in safe historical roles. But there was local pride that Wilson had been born in Staunton in 1856, and in 1940 his birthplace, gussied up considerably from its original state as a Presbyterian manse, was opened as a public shrine with President Franklin D. Roosevelt making the dedicatory address. I was there with my new Brownie camera and when Mrs. Cordell Hull swept me past the Secret Service, I snapped a blurred shot of the back of FDR's noble head.

But before that, Mrs. Edith Bolling Galt Wilson had presented the 1916 Pierce-Arrow to the city, and the city kept it in the tabernacle, and then in the cellar of the local Buick agency where I saw it supporting one wall of the coal bin. During the Woodrow Wilson Centennial of 1956, they dragged out the gigantic black limousine to carry Mrs. Wilson in Staunton's triumphal parade. The old Pierce was dingy, dented, and moth-ravaged in its viscera. After a heroic struggle, it started issuing loud, rude, flatulent backfires, and with a final puff of white smoke, died in front of the Dixie Theater. A gracious, laughing Mrs. Wilson was escorted into a less historic vehicle for the parade finale.

By 1979, the twenty-eighth president had long receded into his historical portrait as the Woodrow Wilson Foundation completed a fresh, second restoration of "The Birthplace," as it's called in Staunton. The job was said to reflect more accurately the Spartan truth of 1856 and the old Pierce, put back into as-new condition, reposed elegantly in its garage at the foot of the Birthplace garden.

History and its supporting artifacts had been treasured up, put right, assigned proper places. We have to do it. Virginians do it better than almost anybody. Each generation loses some preservation battles (I still mourn Mr. Bryan's Fiat) and wins some. But just before the dry-freezing process of certified, mild Shintoism occurs, there's a fleeting time of fun and danger and uncertainty. Breaking down in a parade, the battered old Pierce-Arrow had a charm it lost when all the honest scars of time were wiped away.

* * *

Virginia has all the subtleties of any border region. Some of the parts that seem so placid and picturesque today actually have turbulent histories. Staunton, in the center of the Shenandoah Valley, developed at the approximate center of the 175-mile-long basin, at the intersection of two important early trails. Indians, immigrants, armies, merchants, and tourists combined over the centuries to make Staunton a rather sophisticated little city, with several ethnic influences.

One result was a mixture of accents. Glottologically the town is chaotic. Strangled vowels of the Scotch-Irish, the harsh patois of early Germans filtered through Pennsylvania, and the soft, hushpuppy idiom of the eastern Virginia English (and black offshoots) have endured individually and combined since the 1730s. I can tell the special central Shenandoah Valley sound, I can hear it in the lyrics of those sweet-warbling Stauntonians, the Statler Brothers. But I can't explain it.

There is one singular pronunciation common to nearly all Virginians but those of the far southwest. It's the way we say house, about, grout, tout, and pout. Contrary to scurrile falsehood, we do *not* say HOOSE, ABOOT, and so forth. What we do say is impossible to spell phonetically, but HEAOUSE and ABEAOUT — said quickly, with no drawl — come close. As far as I have observed, the only other North Americans who talk thus are Anglo-Canadians. Occasional published reports claim to have discovered a time capsule of mountain-locked Virginians still spouting pure Elizabethan dialect. I have been up far hollows where they still say "hit" for it, but I never heard any chatter that sounded Elizabethan.

Nor was I ever privy to the legendary conflict between Shenandoah Valley people (and their close mountain cousins) to which tribe Woodrow Wilson and I belonged, and eastern Virginians, across the Blue Ridge. That had faded long before. The Civil War, with its partitioning of West Virginia, removed those counties which had the least in common with the rest of us, and that helped end some famous bickering. Even the old names "Cohees" and "Tuckahoes" faded away as derisive terms.

Some time in the late 1930s I made my first trip across the mountain to the east. That is, if you have been following the geographical clues in this personal introduction to Virginia, the Blue Ridge. What a wonderful mountain! Without it, Virginia's geography would be hopelessly confusing. Even with that careful, tidy verge marking east from west, there's trouble finding coherence in our various regions.

There's no question when you reach salt

At Newport News, fervor of a James River baptism grips a congregation from the United House of Prayer for All People.

water, though, and to this day the spectacular, heavenly stench of crab in Virginia's fishing ports takes me back to that first trip to eastern Virginia and to Irvington, a Chesapeake Bay town at the mouth of the Rappahannock River. From a boat called a deadrise I fished with a hand line for spot and croaker. Blowtoads and stinging nettles swam into my life for the first time. But my most vivid memory deals with the abandoned sailing ships that lay rotting in various Tidewater inlets. It seemed that coastal Virginia was one vast graveyard for schooners, sloops, bugeyes, and other once-graceful relics shoved up a creek to let nature take its course.

I dredge up that memory because it links me personally with one of Virginia's great modern mysteries. In the late 1970s, reports began surfacing from that same area concerning dark, humpy, sinuous creatures swimming in the water. Sea monsters — one of the few assets Virginia had lacked—finally were here. Most of the reports came from the lower Potomac, where the river is enormously wide as it flows the last few miles into Chesapeake Bay. Some of the monster-spotting occurred from lookouts near the ancient plantation homes of the Washingtons and the Lees, thus investing the monster story with scrupulous Virginia protocol.

Indeed, many citizens reported seeing "Chessie," and they weren't all drunk or seeking publicity. When you got down to basics, the reports were pretty much alike. What they were describing was a big snake. That gave birth to the anaconda theory. It is technically possible that anacondas — giant South American snakes traveling in the hulls of sailing ships — entered Virginia waters when the ships were abandoned in the 1930s. The largest Chessie was estimated to be some thirty-odd feet long. Anacondas are known to reach thirty-seven feet.

* * *

Chimeras in the tributaries or not, Chesapeake Bay dominates eastern Virginia as mountains dominate the west. James Michener's novel dealt mainly with the upper, or Maryland, portion. Virginia's part is wider but shorter, and controls the small mouth which opens on the Atlantic, through which—to give you an idea of its importance to commerce — comes all the shipping for

Gentle ogre of the forest, a box turtle plods its timeless rounds in a Virginia lowland wilderness.

Baltimore up north, Virginia's Hampton Roads complex down south, and lesser ports like Richmond and Alexandria.

Any understanding of how eastern Virginia was settled, and why its towns are where they are, must be based on water. Even before the first European settlements, the bay was correctly perceived as gateway to many safe harbors beyond the Atlantic's reach, to fertile land for settling, and to rivers leading into the interior and — such was the naive hope — even the fabled passage to India. Here, on the banks of the great bay and its rivers, the European culture splashed ashore no later than 1559.

I like the fact that so much of Virginia's shore — indeed, almost all its oceanfront — remains nearly as unspoiled today as then. The fragile-looking peninsula that forms the bay's eastern edge, the Eastern Shore, also provides most of Virginia's actual oceanfront. Luckily for the biosphere's preservation, Virginia's version of land's end is difficult to find. You can hardly get there from here. An overwhelming majority of Virginians, and even 40 percent of Eastern Shore residents, never get there at all.

I didn't get there — to the wild island shore — until last year. Here is what I found, at the very door to Virginia.

Picture a perfect beach of about sixty miles. Break it now and then with a narrow inlet, a sly diplomatic concession to the Atlantic, blustering endlessly on its front. Strew the broad sands (at least 100 yards of it before the first line of dunes) with shells. Spangle the air with rare birds. Omit homo sapiens.

Hard to believe, I thought, standing on this untracked sand with no trace of mankind in any direction, that such a place lay 100 miles southeast of Washington, D.C., and 20 miles from Norfolk. The Virginia Barrier Islands, which form this marvel, are the last intact, unaltered island chain off the eastern United States. They may comprise the coast's last bastion of clean water and healthy seafood.

Once, in the national dawn, we settled these islands. Some claim that Edward (Blackbeard) Teach, the eminent pirate, was a native or part-time resident. Much later, unrestricted sport and market hunting savaged the bird population. But the ocean drove us out, and while the birds may never return in their former number, today's flocks of feathered migrants, wintering visitors, and permanent residents are spectacular. Among the dozens of species are snow geese, black duck, glossy ibis, whistling swan, and ten species of hawks. One, the peregrine falcon, is on the endangered list. The beauty part is that here, at least, the danger should be over. Quietly, in the 1970s, The Nature Conservancy bought thirteen of the eighteen islands that comprise the Virginia barriers. The others are deemed in safe hands. The less-adventurous can get a sample of the setting by driving to the northernmost ocean island, Assateague, which is the only one accessible by car. It connects by bridge to the fishing village of Chincoteague. Assateague's famed wild ponies still graze, potbellied, through the national wildlife refuge they call home.

Crossing from the Eastern Shore to the Virginia mainland, the traveler drives southward out to sea on the seventeen-mile Chesapeake Bay Bridge-Tunnel. When he strikes land at Virginia Beach, modern Tidewater Virginia is at hand. But even here, sanctuaries of stunning natural beauty remain. Take Seashore State Park, about 3,000 acres at the tip of Cape Henry.

Seashore, because of some freakish combination of heat and humidity, is the northernmost outpost of abundant Spanish moss. In great festoons it sways from stately bald cypress trees, like the beards of assembled Chinese patriarchs. The bald cypress itself is no commonplace Virginia tree, and the dark swamp waters at their knees, the color of a weak Bourbon highball, strike me as more suitable for the deep South. Yet it was here, in such an atypical Virginia setting, that the nation's first permanent English-speaking settlers came ashore.

You've heard the basic Jamestown story? Well, two weeks before the settlers reached Jamestown, their three ships — Susan Constant, Godspeed, and Discovery — anchored just beyond the surf off Cape Henry. It was April 26, 1607. The pioneers saw only "white hilly sand." Coming ashore, they found "faire meaddowes and goodly tall trees, with such fresh waters running through the woods" that the Englishmen were "almost ravished." A reception committee of Indians was running through the woods as well, "their Bowes in their mouthes." They fell upon the landing party, wounded two, and drove the white men back to their ships. In the best tradition of adventure novels, the English opened a box of sealed orders and sailed away—for an appointment with destiny at Jamestown.

Could those pioneers return to Cape Henry today, their ships would be dwarfed by giant colliers, as many as 125 anchored in stately rows, waiting their turns at the Hampton Roads coal piers. Looking to shore, the explorers would see the bright nylon tents of campers, and the Beetle Bailey architecture of a small, misplaced Army camp. They would see Old Cape Henry Lighthouse, funded by the first U.S. Congress and built in 1791, and New Cape Henry Lighthouse, now 100 years old. They would see miles of beachfront hotels. But they would also see dunes and live oaks and cypress swamps, where pileated woodpeckers bejewel gray veils of Spanish moss.

Virginia Beach is a vast land anchor securing the state's southeast. The beachfront hotel/boardwalk strip takes up only a small part; most of the area is agricultural, military, and residential in character, with some careful development of clean industry. Many Beach people work in adjoining Norfolk, Virginia's largest city, whose downtown rehabilitation over the past twenty years has astonished the world. For uncounted preceding generations the old port was known by an unprintable nickname until, suddenly, the gamy heart of it all, East Main Street, was bashed to rubble. Gone were the reeking bars and arcades, the burlesque theater, the tattoo parlors and cheap rooms: all the raucous accessories required — or so it always seemed — by shady women and boisterous men. All gone. Then, with comparable speed, the new highrises went up, and Norfolk was a vista of malls, fountains, glass, and a luxury waterfront hotel.

Mercifully, Norfolk saved a few jewels from prior incarnations, like the Moses Myers House of 1792. That's one of the finest early Federal townhouses ever built in America. Myers was one of America's first millionaires, and a man of great taste. His original furnishings and collections remain largely intact.

The sea has always ruled Norfolk. But there was one American soldier who upstaged the Navy there, and that was General Douglas MacArthur. Converting an antebellum courthouse, he chose the city for his

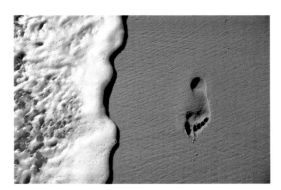

Spanish in 1559, English in 1607, tourists in the 1980s. Virginia's coast remembers—for a moment.

monumental tomb. Norfolk was his "home by choice," the great general said, even though he had been accidentally born in Arkansas "while his parents were away." Like him, the MacArthur Memorial blends dignity with a touch of solid theater. It is a center of scholarship with its vast archives, as well as the repository of such colorful MacArthur relics as his characteristic cap, corncob pipe, and sunglasses.

Another Norfolk surprise came when Walter P. Chrysler, Jr., decided to adopt the city as home for his massive art collection. Renamed the Chrysler Museum, Norfolk's fine arts museum became permanent home to some of the world's masterpieces. It is particularly strong in French Impressionists.

Norfolk suffered cruelly during the Revolution (as it would again in the Civil War) and the city has saved one melodramatic souvenir of the war's opening salvo. Lord Dunmore, Virginia's despised royal governor, had fled Williamsburg and boarded a gun-

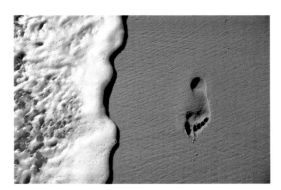

Resplendent in pinks, a master of foxhounds leads an autumn hunt near Middleburg.

boat of the British fleet in Norfolk harbor. On New Year's Day of 1776, he commanded the bombardment that would destroy a third of the city, and warrant his ineffaceable knavery among Norfolkians. In the process, one of Dunmore's cannonballs struck the brick tower of St. Paul's Church. It smacked deeply into the masonry but remained clearly visible, protruding slightly like a dark boil.

A few years ago Lord Louis Mountbatten, World War II leader and last viceroy of India, was taken on a tour of Norfolk sights. An accompanying gaggle of local VIPs nudged each other as they gathered before the tower, and the guide related and embellished the story of Dunmore's villainy. Then they waited, muffling smirks, for Mountbatten's response. With an old gunner's eye, he surveyed the British cannonball's off-center position in the tower, then snorted disgustedly:

"Hmmf. Damn near missed it, didn't he?"

Looking around the broad and busy Norfolk harbor we find no views the first explorers would recognize. Here the time machine breaks down. No green shore remains. Military jets, great brawny darts, roll shrieking over the colliers and carriers that rest on Hampton Roads' vast flatness. Approaching the main harbor tunnel by car, skimming along a low causeway just above the whitecaps, is a breathtaking sight. Ships as large as mountains ride at anchor, or move ponderously, blocking the horizon. Occasionally, the ink-black hull of a nuclear sub slithers out to sea.

We dip into the tunnel and pop forth quickly on the Hampton side. Look, off to the right, that's Fort Monroe, the U.S. Army's last active moated fort. I do not wax sentimental over military bases. They trail in memory like a dismal phalanx of indistinguishable barracks and overheated orderly rooms. But Fort Monroe is something special. Long predating the Civil War, it was later a Union Army stronghold in the heart of the Confederacy. After the war, the Yankees imprisoned Jeff Davis in one of its casemates. You can see the unaltered cell today. The fort has important associations for black America. Runaway slaves found it a refuge, and called it "Freedom Fort." One reason Hampton Institute —look quickly there, to the left—was founded: the number of blacks clustered

here just after the war. One of them was a young man from far-off Franklin Country, near Roanoke. Working hard at Hampton Institute, Booker T. Washington fitted himself for a great and inspiring career, becoming the leading civil rights figure of his time.

We're almost at the end of the north causeway, There's just time enough for a glance at the Hampton fishing fleet. It was here, at Blackbeard's point, that local hero Captain Maynard sailed home in 1718, the pirate's head impaled on a spike. It's all so hard to picture. Nor can we, looking over toward Newport News, conjure any visions of the pioneer ironclads *Monitor* and *Merrimack*, dueling. There! Just off the point.

The James, that most Virginian of rivers, that perfect stream that springs from a Highland county pasture and traverses the state, ends here, at Newport News, in the harbor called Hampton Roads which gives, in turn, on Chesapeake Bay. The state's other great rivers simply flow into the bay, and thus spawned no additional ports at their mouths. But all the rivers—James, York, Rappahannock, and Potomac—were busy highways, and would create trading centers upstream.

It must have seemed beautiful to the 1607 settlers, searching for a safe place to debark and commence their colony. For seventeen days after their rude rejection by the Indians of Virginia Beach, they sailed the tidal rivers, carefully scouting a likely spot. Finally they agreed on a small peninsula thirty miles up the James River from Hampton Roads.

Let's be charitable. The Englishmen by then were fearful about the entire project. We can hardly blame them for picking a site that was easy to vacate. That's about the best to be said of Jamestown, a spot so close to the river's main channel that ships tied up to trees. The peninsula they had chosen was so low and swampy it was hardly land at all. Much has been made of the fumbling incompetence of the early Jamestowners—Captain John Smith always excepted—and of their stupidity in choosing such a miasmic setting. And yet, from its very selection there still radiates the poignancy of childlike fears. And their fears were realized.

But now with our first permanent English settlers tenuously breathing the marshy air of Jamestown, there comes an awkward detour, or flashback, wherein we stumble over a simple truth about Old Virginia that is customarily avoided.

The Spanish were here first.

"We prefer to begin our history in 1607," snapped James Branch Cabell, the Virginia man of letters who tried, with scant success, to develop the truth about Virginia's first European colonists, unarguably Spanish. Some of our historical markers commemorate not what did happen, Cabell said, but what ought to have happened. Thus we are the children of Smith, John Rolfe, and Pocahontas, and that is that. But Cabell tried hard to dig from obscurity not only the Spaniards, but the name and reputation of the first patriot in Virginia history, an Indian.

In 1559, when some early Spanish explorers landed in Virginia, they were greeted hospitably by local Indians. One of them, a young chief, signed on with the Spaniards. Traveling with them to Havana and Mexico City, he was baptized Luis de Velasco, and sailed for Spain where King Philip II directed his education and gave him a pension. For several years, Virginian Luis de Velasco was a sort of pet in the Spanish court. Then he returned to America in the service of Admiral Pedro Menéndez de Aviles, governor of Florida, and helped Menéndez establish St. Augustine.

In autumn, 1570, still thirty-seven years ahead of the Jamestown English, a Spanish ship sailed north to Chesapeake Bay (they called it Bay of the Mother of God, "the best and largest port in the world") to establish a colony called Ajacán. That first settlement, a Jesuit mission, led by Father Baptista de Segura, totaled only ten people—including Luis de Velasco. Menéndez had promised to send a supply ship in the spring with more settlers. Meantime, the party would spend the winter proselytizing.

But in the dead of winter, when there was no chance of a Spanish ship awkwardly appearing, Don Luis de Velasco turned to his fellow Virginia Indians and ordered the massacre of the Jesuits. Only one, a boy named Alonso, was spared.

With spring came the promised relief expedition, full of plans to buttress Virginia's first permanent European colony. But when the Spanish finally located Alonso and heard his ghastly story, they slaughtered an appropriate number of Indians and returned to Florida. Apparently they made no further serious efforts to settle Virginia.

Cabell concluded that Don Luis had seen in Mexico, Cuba, and Florida what happened to native Americans when the Spaniard took over. Luis sought to spare his people a fate of decimation and enslavement, and thus, Cabell decided, became the first patriot in Virginia history. If he had not exterminated the Jesuits, the colony — reinforced in 1571 — might well have thrived. The Spanish were skilled colonizers. Not just Virginia, but the whole of the Atlantic seaboard between Chesapeake Bay and Florida could have been Spanish.

Later research, not available to Cabell, slightly diminishes his portrait of the noble Virginia Indian who made a pre-emptive strike in an act of conscious patriotism. Two Jesuit scholars, Clifford M. Lewis and Albert J. Loomie, found Spanish archival material that confirmed the basic story and revealed a volatile, fast-talking streak in Velasco, who may have been merely homesick for Virginia and the rightful harem to which, as a polygamous chief, he was entitled. Worse, once he reached home, he may have feloniously coveted the communion silver and vestments of the Jesuits.

It is hard to say, and we'll probably never know. But whatever the reason, Velasco squelched the Spanish in Virginia. Cabell thought he led his tribe to safety in the western mountains; later research found no indication of that.

Cabell placed the Spanish colony on the Northern Neck between the Potomac and the Rappahannock. Lewis and Loomie definitely established that the initial Spanish landing was near Jamestown, on the James, which they called the River of the Holy Spirit, and that the actual colony was established across the lower peninsula, near present Yorktown. There Luis de Valasco, Virginia patriot or perfidious murderer, or both, vanished safely amid the oaks and pines.

Seventeen years would pass before Velasco's patron, Phillip II, hurled his Armada against the hated English. Another generation would rise before Cervantes began writing Don Quixote in the Sevilla jail. William Shakespeare was a lad of seven.

*   *   *

The English colonization would have its share of false starts, too, including disasters for would-be settlers Sir Humphrey Gilbert and Sir Walter Raleigh. But in 1606 King James granted a charter to the London Company, whose stockholders hungered for the discovery of precious metals and a short cut to the South Seas. In picking personnel for the historic 1607 expedition, the company fathers chose wisely in the sole case of Captain John Smith.

By year's end, more than half the 100 English men and boys planted at Jamestown were dead. Survivors thrashed about the wilderness, pathetically trying to honor the parent company's demands for gold and Pacific passage. Only the election of squat, stormy John Smith as president of the ruling council gave the Jamestowners the discipline they needed to survive.

But soon Smith, badly injured, was packed off to England for medical treatment, and the winter of 1609-10, known through Virginia history as the Starving Time, persuaded the entire colony to abandon the town. Sailing down the James, they nearly reached Hampton Roads before encountering an inbound ship with supplies and new settlers. The weary veterans turned back, little realizing, or caring, that they had just saved Jamestown's reputation as America's first permanent English speaking settlement.

Around 1612, settler John Rolfe began experimenting with tobacco, and by 1614 — when he married the Indian girl Pocahontas —he had begun shipping leaf to England. By 1619, tobacco had become the colony's most important export. The futile search for gold officially ended, though King James did not care for tobacco, and described it in terms today's anti-smokers would approve: "A custome lothsome to the eye, hateful to the nose, harmfull to the braine, dangerous to the lungs, and in the blacke stinking fume thereof, neerest resembling the horrible Stygian smoke of the pit that is bottomlesse."

But smoke was a success, and so was Virginia's first interracial marriage. When Powhatan's favorite daughter, fun-loving Pocahontas, married Rolfe, she was wise beyond her teenage years, a gamine who bridged the gulf between settler and native. The union bought a few years of peace, although she was soon dead, on a trip to

England, of white man's disease. Five years later, a ghastly Indian massacre wiped out one-third of the colony.

Today, at Jamestown, the shape of all those memories seems close yet elusive, like the glimpse of a branch swaying at some creature's passage in the silent woods. Little has changed along the low and marshy James bank. Erosion has lopped off the site of the original fort, but you can walk amid the foundation ruins of the settlers' houses, and stand inside the church tower of 1639. Two memorable statues recall two immortal personalities: restless, unconquerable Smith, glaring out across the tan tide of the lower James; Pocohontas, stepping lightly from the forest, about to smile a welcome, hands outstretched. Most visitors touch her hand. It is an informal and lovely setting, amid crape myrtles and pecan trees, free of fear and violence. The National Park Service visitor center does a masterful job of archeological displays and interpretation. The state of Virginia maintains a reconstruction of the original fort and crude buildings, as well as full-size replicas of the three pioneering ships. But there is somehow a sense of melancholy departure at Jamestown. The legends are fixed. The clamors, far away.

*　　*　　*

What a different story ten miles up the road at Williamsburg!

Virginians look upon their old capital as both a spiritual and temporal home. We never dismiss Williamsburg as a tourist attraction. We like nothing better than a trip there, restoring ourselves in Chowning's Tavern, The King's Arms, or Christiana Campbell's. We stroll Duke of Gloucester Street and hungrily sniff the air. We think Williamsburg is how the entire country ought to look, and we always leave it reluctantly, vaguely troubled by the suspicion that since 1740 architecture and ambience everywhere else have been sliding downhill.

Back in the 1920s, the Reverend W. A. R. Goodwin, rector of Bruton Parish Church, was convinced the sleepy, almost-forgotten town still retained much of its original character behind altered and battered facades. Somehow, he conveyed the vision to John D. Rockefeller, Jr., who proved to be an ideal patron of Colonial Williamsburg. Rockefeller was not just immensely wealthy.

He had the taste, leadership, and unflagging interest to personally guide the restoration for more than thirty years.

The restoration, Rockefeller once reflected, "offered an opportunity to restore a complete area and free it entirely from alien or inharmonious surroundings as well as to preserve the beauty and charm of the old buildings and gardens of the city and its historic significance. As the work progressed, I have come to feel that perhaps an even greater value is the lesson that it teaches of the patriotism, high purpose, and unselfish devotion of our forefathers to the common good."

The restoration's uncompromising quality and scholarship are plain to the thoughtful visitor. Less obvious is why the result is so esthetically right. There is the architecture, certainly. Most of it we call "Georgian," although some predates even the first George by several monarchs. No matter. The buildings, whether elegant like the Governor's Palace or modest like the milliner's shop, are *right*. We agree on that. But not many Virginians understand a fundamental truth about Williamsburg: it was a carefully planned community.

The chief designer, Lieutenant Governor Francis Nicholson, drew off a careful pattern of wide streets, ample lots, precise setbacks, open vistas, and public greens. The main street, Duke of Gloucester, extended nearly a mile between the College of William and Mary to the west, and the capitol to the east. In 1699, the capital moved from Jamestown, as though to make a clean break with the unlucky first capital before the eighteenth century arrived. If it was a luck-courting gesture, it worked. Williamsburg would be a fortunate place, prospering as the political, social, and cultural center of a colony that stretched west and north to the Mississippi and the Great Lakes. In 1780, during the Revolution, the capital was moved to Richmond, where it would stay. Williamsburg began its long slumber.

But the town's eighty-one years in eighteenth century limelight spanned Virginia's golden age. The years brought to town such men as William Byrd II, George Washington, Patrick Henry, Francis Fauquier, Thomas Jefferson, Alexander Spotswood, George Mason, George Wythe, Richard

Henry Lee, and the wretched Lord Dunmore. We sense their presence and their conflicts. The visitor becomes aware of political principles that took root and flourished here centuries ago. Awareness of individual worth and dignity, and the concepts of responsible leadership, self-government, liberty, and economic opportunity seem soaked into the very ground along Duke of Gloucester Street.

The College of William and Mary was a powerful influence on the era's intellectual ferment. Students like Jefferson, James Monroe, and John Marshall sprang from the classrooms of such distinguished faculty as physicist William Small and jurist Wythe.

William and Mary predates even Williamsburg. Chartered in 1693, it is the second oldest college in the United States. The cornerstone of its first structure was laid in 1695. Today, the Wren Building, amazingly preserved, remains the heart and flagship of the handsome campus.

Almost ninety of the town's buildings are original; hundreds more are reconstructed on original foundations. Early in the restoration, discovery of two original documents made the job easier and assured its accuracy. The "Frenchman's Map" of 1782, drawn by one of Rochambeau's engineers after the battle of Yorktown, was a marvel of verisimilitude, featuring a tiny scale outline of every building in town. The "Bodleian Plate" was a copperplate engraving of about 1740, discovered at Oxford University. It provided essential architectural detail of the Governor's Palace, the capitol, and the Wren Building, and archeological evidence erupted from the earth.

Study the small details. In vignettelike freeze-frames we pierce the veil of time, learning in precious fragments just how the eighteenth century looked, sounded, and smelled. Imagination, though it helps, is not required. We do not need to speculate on the tonal signature of the noonday gun, or the smell of its burnt cannon powder puffing white across market square. We know. Just as we know the fragrance of cookies baking in a tavern kitchen, or a bowl of fresh-cut flowers in George Wythe's front hall.

Museums are fine, but sometime misleading. We spy a solitary artifact, cast up from some ancient time, and say: how remarkable. Yet removed from its life cycle or di-

Money crop: patient hand labor still pays in the tobacco belt's hot fields.

vorced from other interacting elements of an extinct process, it may be hard to understand. Not so at Williamsburg. The candlemaker stays busy manufacturing candles. The weaver weaves, the printer prints, the cooper coops, and the blacksmith torments his sullen, glowing iron. More than a score of such trades are worked by hundreds of masters, journeymen, and apprentices.

One of my favorites is the gunsmith shop. Its former master, Wallace Gusler, discovered that some of the most beautiful long rifles — theretofore attributed to Pennsylvania — were made in Virginia. They invariably reflected a sublime sense of taste and proportion often lacking in the sometimes gaudy, fashion-prone Pennsylvania specimens.

Expanding his horizons, Gusler applied his detectivelike methods to eighteenth century furniture, proving that masterpieces thought to have sprung from shops in Philadelphia and Boston were positively accredited to master hands in Williamsburg, Norfolk, and Fredericksburg. This information caused a minor sensation, particularly among Virginia collectors, who for generations had been told that nothing but simple cottage furniture ever came from Virginia craftsmen.

These days, in such Williamsburg shops as the gunsmith's and the cabinetmaker's, the real thing takes form once more. A year's production at the gunsmith's shop is about six rifles. But the guns are secondary, says Master Gary Brumfield. "We talk to more than a quarter-million people a year in this shop, demonstrating the trade. Education is what we're making; guns are a by-product." Some by-product. The cheapest all-handmade rifle is $7,700, and you'll have to wait ten to twelve years for delivery. The most expensive, highly-ornamented rifle runs $12,000. "Loaded, all options," laughs the red-bearded master gunsmith.

In 1975 a construction worker stringing fence just outside Williamsburg saw something at the base of an oak tree. He reached down and touched the perfectly preserved brass hilt of a saber, its blade buried in the ground. Dug out, it was pitted but intact. The worker thoughtfully carried it to a nearby archeologist, who was delighted by the rare sight of a French grenadier briquet, model 1767. In Virginia, the touch of France is much like the saber: elusive yet discoverable. Cer-

tainly, Jefferson and other Revolutionary era leaders were drenched in the views of *Philosophes* like Voltaire.

And it was highly practical French help that brought the Revolution to such a stunning conclusion at nearby Yorktown. Coming when needed, doing everything right, the Comte de Rochambeau, the Marquis de Lafayette, and the Comte de Grasse helped end the siege of Yorktown in the colonials' favor. It was no Armageddon as battles go, but back in England, Prime Minister Lord North, hearing the news cried, "Oh God! It is all over," and resigned.

Yorktown (the third point of Virginia's Historic Triangle, with Jamestown and Williamsburg) is nearly unaffected by the march of two centuries. The town was already in decline at the time of the Revolution, and little has occurred since. The battlefield is almost as it was in 1781. You can stroll though trenches and redoubts, and see cannon-scarred houses that survived the battle. Out in the broad York River, where Cornwallis' fleet burned, marine archeologists dive patiently in Stygian muck.

Virginia's navigable eastern rivers were the chief arteries of travel and commerce, which is why all the great eighteenth century plantations face their respective rivers, instead of to the rear, where highways could come later. The lower James River plantations formed a notable cluster. Carter's Grove, often nominated the most beautiful house in America, lies just downstream from Williamsburg and is owned by the Restoration.

Virginia's golden age, often dated by the two middle quarters of the eighteenth century, saw the construction of most of the great plantations that remain today. Halfway between Williamsburg and Richmond lies the perfect trio of Berkeley, Shirley, and Westover plantations. Strangely untouched by time, the culture they preserve is no antebellum Dixie, cotton-and-columns tableau, aplunk with banjos. Clustered within a few miles of each other beside the silent, ocher James, they endure in a style so grand and difficult that only their owners' ferocious commitments sustain it. Beauty and independence are paid for by each generation, as if renewing the builders' pride and virile entrepreneurship. If you think Virginia's plantation people spend their time hunting foxes, im-

bibing juleps, and thumping their canes, you just haven't met them.

"It's a trust," says Frederick S. Fisher III of Westover, built by the legendary William Byrd II. "You're given this to see what you can do with it. I'm a custodian here."

At Shirley, C. Hill Carter, Jr., is the ninth generation in a string of unbroken ownership that goes back to 1660. Later, Robert (King) Carter was a giant of early Virginia; Ann Hill Carter married "Light Horse" Harry Lee and brought her child, Robert E. Lee, back home for visits. Today, in frayed khakis, Shirley's hard-working squire is mistaken for a hired man by tourists coming to see his rare estate.

Malcolm Jamieson, owner of Berkeley, took over the derelict plantation in 1929, and spent the next half-century reviving it and learning about Berkeley's incredible history: a signer of the Declaration and a U.S. President were born here; the nation's first Thanksgiving service was mandated here as an annual event, in 1619; *Taps* was composed and first played here when McClellan encamped 100,000 on the grounds after The Seven Days; and just possibly the first bourbon whiskey was distilled here.

In the twenty years I have known Mac Jamieson, I believe he's done the equivalent of three lifetimes of hard labor. But at seventy-one, he is barely slowing down, and son Jamie, thirty-six, already has the weathered, massive hands of a veteran farmer. "The only way we'd ever sell would be by going bankrupt," Jamie says, "We struggle. We give it our all. But it's very satisfying. We don't

In Williamsburg, wigmaking is one of many eighteenth century trades now revived and displayed.

Thoroughbreds test the fog-dampened grass near Jefferson's Charlottesville.

understand sitting back on inherited wealth."

I wouldn't claim such people are totally representative of Virginia gentry, but they set some powerfully good examples for the rest.

* * *

One of the many accomplishments of William Byrd II — that supremely cultivated eighteenth century aristocrat, builder of Westover, explorer of far wilderness, dallier in London salons, poet, lawyer, politician, and exploiter of chambermaids — was the proper founding of the city of Richmond in 1733. Before that, probably for more than 100 years, it had been a rude trading post. The navigable James ended there in a mass of rapids at the fall line, the visible boundary marking Tidewater from Piedmont. With efficient bulk transportation ending at the first riffle, trading centers like Alexandria on the Potomac, Fredericksburg on the Rappahannock, and Petersburg on the Appomattox also sprang up. As the colony's population increased and its security improved, Virginians began spilling into higher ground beyond the fall line. The action was cultivated by such prominant colonials as Byrd, who saw upland Virginia as a ripe economic opportunity. There was no significant break in the culture between Tidewater and Piedmont: the same people expanded west and continued planting tobacco.

Thanks to the interstates, the views offered incoming visitors to the old Byrd II trading post are spectacular from two directions. To those approaching by I-95 from the south, Richmond resembles the city of Oz, a shining vertical mass. The image is enhanced by three new skyscrapers: the silver tower of the Federal Reserve Bank juts upward from the southernmost position on the James bank; behind it stands Virginia Electric and Power Company's new buff-colored building; then, a mass of banks and office buildings shoots off to the right, ending in the state government's newest extravaganza, a distinguished beige tower of fluted corners, the tallest building in Virginia.

The other good view is enjoyed by drivers approaching from the east on I-64. Here the skyline is more complex: not as vertical, and darker, somberer in color, close-up of a middle-sized American city, as if seen through a 135 mm lens.

Against such backdrops, it's hard to picture

anything that happened before last week. But there is another view of Richmond, better than any other, which the casual traveler never sees. This is the one from the brow of Church Hill, looking west, across Shockoe Valley, the odd little chasm which has divided Richmond since its earliest days. Back in the 1830s and 40s, this was the view favored by artists and lithographers. The composition was handy, dramatic, and covered most of the city. Dominating the scene, just across Shockoe Valley, was the Capitol, completed in 1792.

To this spot, on April 3, 1865, came Mathew Brady with his photographic equipment. By coordinating a series of abutting views, he made four exposures which, printed carefully together, made a stunning panorama of Richmond. In addition to sheer photographic excellence, there are some other reasons why the view is both important and poignant.

Over the financial district at left center, the picture is clouded by smoke. This can only be from the evacuation fire, caused when retreating Confederates fired their military storehouses to destroy tobacco and other useful commodities. The fire spread, and destroyed much of the city's heart. Charred walls and chimneys stand in the distance beneath the smoke. Consider that when Brady made this picture the war was still in progress. Even then Lee was retreating through the mud of Southside Virginia, on the road to Appomattox. One more great battle, Sayler's Creek, remained to be fought. Thus, the Brady photograph is a look at the eve of destruction. And what heightens its sense of dread and unreality is that nowhere in these clear, open streets, nowhere on these neat porches, in these yards or stable lots, nowhere in all this bizarre panorama of a great city at the very nadir of its history is there a solitary living figure.

It is a phenomenon unexplained by the long shutter speeds of 1865, in which movement resulted in ghostly, imprecise images. In other candid shots of the era, a few of God's creatures show up. But the haunting cityscape of 1865 tells us something else. Many people had fled, "refugeed," in the term of the time. Those who remained must have hidden inside, peering through curtains with red-rimmed eyes.

With that singular moment in mind, the visitor now seeks out the precise spot, on Grace Street, on Church Hill, and views the scene today. Across Shockoe Valley, where the Capitol dominated the 1865 view, a solid wall of buildings — state government, medical college, banks — rises gleaming in the west. If you know just where to look, a fragment of the Capitol peeps through the modern towers. If you study a bit more, a handful of other ancient survivors, dwarfed by their neighbors, also appear: a church or two, the Confederate White House, and down in the valley some crumbling warehouses where the Alabamians and Georgians maintained military hospitals.

So the scene has changed almost entirely. It is as foreign to the Brady photo as the backside of the moon. And yet, the most astonishing thing of all, in some whimsical way the city has preserved its essential character. The patterns of growth manifested in 1865 must have been determined by some organic destiny, like genes. Certainly, the geography of river, hills, and shallow valleys warrants continuity, but in more subtle ways, most of the business, warehouse, and financial distribution is identical to antebellum times, despite near-total rebuilding.

And some of Richmond's residential districts are true time capsules. The Widow Shelton's home, a tall, Greek Revival town house, resembles scores built in the 1830s and 40s. It was here that poet and author Edgar Allan Poe paid his last known social — and perhaps romantic — call. He visited Elmira Shelton, took the train to Baltimore, and died.

Richmonders are a bit ambiguous about Poe. Not that they aren't proud of him; the city, despite its conservatism, has managed to tolerate eccentricity with a certain grace. But although he grew up in Richmond, and did some of his best work here as editor of the *Southern Literary Messenger*, he wasn't a native. He also wandered and worked in other cities. Poe himself affixed a confusing, tentative P.S. on his civic loyalty oath by stating: "I am a Virginian. At least I call myself one." In a mournful paradox, Poe's mother, a Bostonian, managed to die and be buried in Richmond, whereas Poe's remains still moulder in Baltimore.

The only major historical *faux pax*

Ferns lace the slopes of Virginia's highest mountains in the Mount Rogers National Recreation Area.

Richmonders cannot bear with equanimity is ignorance about the Patrick Henry speech. *The* Patrick Henry speech demanding "Liberty or Death." It was delivered, in 1741, in a Richmond church called St. John's, right across from the Widow Shelton's.

In the way of many immigrants, it seems to be newcomers who get caught up in preservation causes. In Richmond, a few sturdy locals, like the legendary Mary Wingfield Scott, have been joined by naturalized Richmonders bringing fresh perspectives and unoccupied money. One, Andrew J. Asch, Jr., manufacturer and New York native, came to Richmond in the 1950s, liked it, and stayed. In the late 1960s a real estate man showed him the Commodities Exchange Building of 1871 in a neighborhood called Shockoe Slip. In the old building's cavernous board room, blackboards bore the nineteenth century chalkings of wheat and corn prices. The place had been unused for generations. Asch, fascinated, bought the building, "not knowing what I was going to do with it." Then he bought more decayed buildings nearby, all of them tucked neatly between the river and the financial district. Soon he owned a significant part of the neighborhood, and suddenly, as if by spontaneous combustion, Shockoe Slip took off in the 1970s as a fashionable restaurant, shopping, and apartment district. Carefully avoiding the sleaze of "old towns" elsewhere, by 1980 Shockoe Slip was in many ways the heart of Richmond.

Probable location of the first seventeenth century traders' settlement, its name of shadowy Indian origin, Shockoe Slip was destroyed in the fire, and was rebuilt only to decay. Now it's back again. Richmond is taking on the qualities of an Asia Minor settlement where half–a–dozen cities have risen and fallen on the same tormented earth.

Until early in the nineteenth century, Petersburg — just twenty miles south — was Richmond's equal. It, too, began as an important trading center in the 1600s; fared reasonably well in the 1700s; was important enough to rate pillaging by Benedict Arnold; and then boomed after the Revolution. By the 1850s Petersburg was a nationally known center of business, finance, manufacturing, and transportation, and the Petersburgers exacted their due share. With the profits, they

installed gas lights, splendid new commercial buildings, and town mansions. Amid a cityscape of uncommon beauty, Petersburg blossomed socially and culturally. The town's seminaries and academies were notable for quality. Pioneer labor movements and medical associations forecast the future. The highest percentage of free blacks of any Virginia city resided there; its black community produced Joseph Jenkins Roberts, first president of Liberia. Such was the thriving little city in 1861, at the zenith of its wealth and elegance.

Four years later the world knew Petersburg as the Graveyard of the Confederacy.

A ten-month siege ("A dream of terror," said one survivor) gripped Petersburg in 1864-65 as the stubborn Grant hammered at Lee's fragile line. It was the longest, deadliest siege ever waged for an American city. Behind it came a peace almost as hard as war, with wounds too deep to heal.

Postwar poverty saw the original town patched up, not rebuilt. And when the twentieth century came, the town simply papered over its old buildings. But by the late 1970s Petersburg realized it had, intact, an entire, downtown cityscape of great age. The city commenced stripping away the alien veneer of more than a century, and like time-lapse photography in reverse, Petersburg took a great leap backward. Today the mansions, townhouses, and commercial structures of the city's golden age are as they were, and a sense of fitness prevails. For anyone interested in Americana and the Civil War, Petersburg is a supreme point of interest.

Fredericksburg, about seventy-five miles north, halfway between Richmond and Washington, makes an identical claim. Regrettably, all that by-passers see from I-95 is an unedifying outskirt, a Great American Roadside of plastic logos. But this is the town where George Washington grew up, John Paul Jones lived, James Monroe practiced law. If Washington ever hurled a Spanish dollar across a river, it was here, on the Rappahannock, and if he did cut down a cherry tree, the chips fell on a Washington family farm just outside town.

A fall line trading center, Fredericksburg was the strategic settlement for an unusually wide-ranging and rich plantation society. The Washingtons, the Lees, and Fitzhughs,

the Lewises, and other powerful families developed Fredericksburg as a center of trade and gaiety that made it famous in the decades just before and after the Revolution. A sample of its former elegance remains at Kenmore, town mansion of Colonel Fielding Lewis and his wife, Betty Washington, only sister of George to reach maturity.

The Rising Sun Tavern, a charming and original 1760 stagecoach inn, hosted the historic meetings that created Virginia's Statute for Religious Liberty. Nearby stands the home where Washington's mother lived her final years, the boxbushes she planted still thriving. Monroe's law office recall the fifth president's years at the bar and later fame in Washington. We appreciate the age of the Hugh Mercer Apothecary Shop when we learn its original proprietor fought in Scotland with Bonnie Prince Charlie, served in the French and Indian War, settled in Fredericksburg on advice from George Washington, and was killed in the Revolution.

Such are some early details of Fredericksburg. I have been fairly emphatic about them, because the city's close identification with the Civil War (in which Fredericksburg changed hands seven times) is so overpowering that the battle scenes in and around the city often beguile the visitor away from the earlier sites. See it all. And that includes Stratford Hall, birthplace of Lee, a plantation of extraordinary architectural and historical interest, and, nearby, Pope's Creek, birthplace of George Washington, where living history demonstrations by the National Park Service breathe life into the eighteenth century. Both plantations lie on the Potomac about thirty miles east of town.

North of Fredericksburg, nearly all Virginia is affected by the orbital pull of Washington, D.C. Housing developments march across the fields where founding fathers hunted fox. Developers and preservationists argue whether to extend Manassas Battlefield Park. Closer to the Potomac, expressways dodge advancing columns of highrises as we approach the Capital Beltway, carotid artery of all life around the federal city.

Washington's apparently unstoppable stimuli of jobs and power have been good to Virginia. Alexandria, Arlington, Fairfax, and Falls Church seem to ride the crest of an endless boom. There are beautiful new buildings, exquisite shops and restaurants, major league entertainment at Wolf Trap Farm Park. It's a bit intimidating to all but regulars, though, and vaguely foreign. We Virginians are disquieted but stimulated by it. Nowhere else are traffic jams so prodigious, salaries so high, and meals so expensive.

There is rich irony on the Potomac's Virginia bank, for here is the authentic home of two of Virginia's greatest heroes, Washington and Lee. Washington's Mount Vernon stands just south of Alexandria. Lee's father, "Light Horse" Harry Lee, had been a young Revolutionary cavalryman, very close to Washington, and one of the first president's staunchest admirers. Young Robert grew up in Alexandria and married Mary Ann Randolph Custis, a great-granddaughter of Martha Washington. The future Confederate chief's happiest days were spent at Arlington House (just north of Alexandria and across the Potomac from Washington), which his wife inherited on her father's death.

When Robert Edward Lee declined command of the Union army at the outbreak of the war, he left Arlington House forever. The federal government seized the property after a duplicitous imposition of illegal taxes, and converted the estate into a vast graveyard. It was a calculated, remorseless act. But the house remains. Its massive, silent Greek portico still contemplates its wonderful view of L'Enfant's city across the Potomac.

Lee, an engineer, would be amazed — perhaps pleased — by the great jets wafting in and out of Washington National on the Virginia shore, skimming the Washington monument. He would marvel at the clumps and stalks of looping freeways, like vascular systems from *Gray's Anatomy*, and he would probably like the new Metro system, connecting Virginia to the District and to Maryland.

If disoriented by such wonders, he could drop into Alexandria and find some of his old haunts essentially unchanged. So, for that matter, could George Washington, should he canter up the nine miles from serene Mount Vernon. His designated pew still waits in lovely Christ Church. The ancient engines of Friendship Fire Company, to whose volunteer corps Washington belonged, stand ready for the alarm that no longer clangs.

Martha Washington's favorite apothecary looks as though it could still produce leeches on call. Gadsby's Tavern dispenses food and hospitality, and at palatial Carlyle House, colonial governors might be meeting with General Edward Braddock to talk over financing the French and Indian War. These buildings anchor a recent explosion of restorations throughout the seven-by-eleven-block heart of the old town, where an amazing total of more than 500 buildings remain from before 1790. For years a rather shabby appendage of Washington, Alexandria suddenly is fashionable again, reveling in its own charm. When a new Holiday Inn went up in the heart of downtown, it was in the style of two hundred years ago.

Thus in numerous crafty ways Old Virginia has prevailed in the very shadow of the federal colossus. The contrast can be delightful, as, on the boundary of Dulles International Airport, another ancient Lee Plantation, Sully, drowses beneath floating 747s, beside Saarinen's control tower, an ebony-topped wand. Dulles marks the beginning of Virginia's horse country, which is about as tradition-bound an institution as we own. In parts of four northern Virginia counties — Fauquier, Loudoun, Prince William, and Fairfax — the fox hunt and horsey life were fixed when young George Washington and his powerful patron, Lord Fairfax, cultivated the chase over their vast acreage. Once sounded, the view halloo never faded from earshot.

The towns of Leesburg, Middleburg, and Warrenton are the chief ornaments of this complex culture that mixed man, fox, horse, and topography. It was fitting that President Theodore Roosevelt, issuing orders that all U.S. Army officers be able to ride 100 miles a day, tested the plan himself with a round-trip to Warrenton. The town, a Mecca for horsemen in 1909 as well, "loudly greeted and cordially welcomed the president." T.R. may have been a Yankee, but by thunder he was a horseman. A still-earlier sense of historical fitness was conveyed by Colonel John Singleton Mosby, whose fast-riding partisan cavalry made the four-county area immortal as "Mosby's Confederacy." The dapper, fearless guerilla settled in Warrenton after the war, and remains today its preeminent hero.

A near-bewildering variety of horse events greets the visitor to Fauquier and Loudoun Counties. One weekend may offer as many as five horse shows, with one or more every weekend from May 1 to Labor Day. The Warrenton Horse Show, founded in 1899, is *the* hunter show of America, and the Warrenton Gold Cup in May is Virginia's top spectator horse attraction and one of the nation's premier steeplechases. A Virginia steeplechase is a pleasantly countrified affair. On a bluegrass-padded hillside you sit with a hamper of sandwiches and a portable bar, watching the horses and riders glide over timber like slow motion animations of antique English horse engravings. Once, at the Warrenton Point-to-Point, I met the comely great-granddaughter of Colonel Mosby.

* * *

South of Warrenton, west of Fredericksburg, Richmond, and Petersburg, Piedmont Virginia spreads like a vast triangle to the Carolina line, its hypotenuse pointing southwest along the Blue Ridge. The state's least-interesting region geographically, Piedmont lacks the drama of the west's mountains, and the grandeur of the east's wide rivers and ocean. But it is drenched in history and a charm of its own. There is ancient melodrama at Danville, where Jefferson Davis and the Confederate cabinet, in full flight after Lee abandoned Petersburg's last ditch, held the last full cabinet meeting and issued the final official Rebel proclamation. More melodrama came to Danville early in this century, when that celebrated fast mail train, Old 97, made her spectacular flight from a Southern Railway trestle into country music immortality.

Here along the border of Tarheelia is tobacco country. The venerable market system still works: in autumn, the fragrant weed is sold in cavernous, scarred warehouses to the lilting chant of the auctioneer, unintelligible to outsiders. But gradually there are changes in this most conservative part of Virginia. In Mecklenburg County, few tobacco farm mules remain to answer the bray of speedboats on Buggs Island Lake, more than eight hundred miles around. On its shore stands a little-known plantation where somebody ought to film a movie. Prestwould was completed in 1795 by an unreconstructed Tory baronet, Sir Peyton Skipwith. His father — Sir William — won the property in a marathon card game from the feckless William Byrd III.

East Coast surfing championships are held annually at the resort city of Virginia Beach.

Today, with its thirty-foot boxwoods, slave-built stone walls, original furnishings, including scenic French wallpaper, and a rare *punkah* in the dining room, Prestwould is a haunted island untouched by time.

Heading north through the Piedmont we encounter industrialized Lynchburg, handsomely situated on hills above the James. It's a prominent college town, too, but it became wider known as headquarters for that paragon of born-again, electronically borne soul shepherds, Jerry Falwell. Nearby, the National Park Service keeps watch on sacred property of another kind, the little village of Appomattox Court House.

All things considered, some make a case that the heart of the Piedmont lies at Charlottesville and surrounding Albemarle County. That would be the view of generations of University of Virginia men, and therefore suspect. But looking at the objective facts, a combination of location plus the temporal reminders of Thomas Jefferson makes the name Jefferson Country a hallmark.

Nowhere in the country does one man, especially one dead more than a century-and-a-half, so dominate a neighborhood. An urbane Frenchman on Rochambeau's staff, the Marquis de Chastellux, visited Jefferson just after the Revolution at his new home, Monticello. A member of the French Academy, a friend of the great leaders of the Enlightenment, Chastellux charmed Williamsburg, and found time to experiment with natural history. In the spring of 1782 he set forth to tour upper Virginia. He found much of interest, but nothing impressed him as much as Thomas Jefferson.

The author of the Declaration of Independence, himself a Francophile and humanist, was not yet forty. He had been governor of Virginia, but in 1782 none could have foretold his future as minister to France, secretary of state, and president. At any rate, the two men formed a lasting friendship, and it is pleasing to speculate that Chastellux in long conversations at Monticello spurred the young American's mind along paths that contributed to his future greatness.

Jefferson had been building Monticello for twelve years. Eventually the house would be a thirty-five room masterpiece on its leveled-off mountaintop, called by many America's most interesting house. Designed in Jefferson's variant on the Palladian style, it is a place of light and harmony and questing intellect. Jefferson's influence was so pervasive it is not surprising to learn he designed Virginia's capitol. But it surprises some that he based it on the Roman temple at Nimes known as the Maison Carrée. Ever the architectural dabbler, Jefferson formulated ideas, then called in Charles Louis Clerrisseau, a French architect, compatible spirit, and expert on Roman archeology, to provide the professional touch. Jefferson and Clerisseau sent back an exquisite scale model in addition to plans.

We can probably credit Jefferson's capitol design with introducing the age of columns to America. Through the 1840s, columns marched vaingloriously across the landscape, especially in deeper Dixie. Virginia, guided by both Jefferson and an aversion to the flamboyant, treated columns with a bit more restraint. Those of Monticello are prominent but integrated into a complex whole that includes the dome and the octagon. Jefferson's final design, the original University of Virginia "academical village" with its pure neo-classical pavilions framing the Rotunda, is an acknowledged *chef d'oeuvre* of American design. The Rotunda was clearly inspired by the Roman Pantheon, heavy and clumsy when compared to Jefferson's exquisite production. The round, domed heart of the campus was nearly destroyed by fire in 1895; famed architect Stanford White, in charge of rebuilding, took some liberties with Jefferson's design, but a restoration in the 1970s put things right. Surrounded by the vast modern university, Jefferson's buildings still afford some of the detached tranquility that he planned.

But loyalists of the university's great rival, William and Mary, always have the last word in any dispute over who has more claim to Jefferson. "Sure, he may have built U-V-A," the William and Mary people say. "But we showed him how."

Before the middle of the nineteenth century, a plethora of architectural revivals moved through the western world, and Virginia escaped none of them: Greek, Roman, Gothic, Egyptian, Italianate. But in our hearts, none of them takes the place of eighteenth century Georgian styles. These days we erect commercial buildings, even entire shopping centers, to slavishly copy the prototypes along Williamsburg's Duke of Gloucester Street. Were Jefferson still at his drawing table it is inconceivable he would be cranking out replicas. He drew very heavily on the past, yet reshaped and experimented to suit himself.

But here is another egregious Virginia quality: preempting Jefferson to support whatever point we're trying to make. We are notorious for it, as bad as the Devil quoting scripture.

Nobody can visit Monticello without a sense of the towering, civilized personality that lived there. And it's exhilarating to stand on Jefferson's beloved little mountain and contemplate the views that he enjoyed. As sunlight sparkles over the bosomy green hills of Albemarle, nourished by a distinctive green limestone, we see a rural landscape of great charm. For generations it was a favorite retreat of wealthy northerners. Impoverished Virginians couldn't keep up the huge estates. Now the wealth has been spread around, but still outsiders hear about Albemarle and buy in.

If, as some say, Charlottesville/Albemarle is the class of Piedmont Virgina, one reason could be its location in the foothills of the Blue Ridge. As William Blake said, "Great things are done when men and mountains meet." In a way, it seems surprising it took Virginians so long to meet their mountains. You'll remember that we left our pioneers of the seventeenth and early eighteenth centuries advancing westward with their tobacco fields.

When they reached the mountains they just stopped.

Looking at the Blue Ridge today — approaching it, say, on the long glide of westbound I-64 near Charlottesville — it is hard to understand why the gentle range intimidated early settlers. You'd think they would have regarded it as an inconvenience worth surmounting, for from the earliest explorations the Shenandoah Valley was clearly fertile and altogether desirable.

In the 1660s the dream of a short cut to Asia still glowed. Virginia's irascible royal governor, William Berkeley, backed German physician John Lederer's offer to seek a pass through the mountains. The governor planned to profit from fur trade, gold and silver discoveries, or the longed-for Asian passage. In spring, 1669, Lederer set forth from the eastern Piedmont, and in ten days scaled the summit of the Blue Ridge. He was probably in today's Madison County. Misled by the haze behind him to the east, he thought he "had a beautiful prospect of the Atlantick Ocean washing the Virginian shore." Ahead, "to the north and west, my sight was suddenly bounded by mountains higher than I stood upon." He tried to find a gap through the crest, failed, and returned to the east, but not before he became the first recorded white man to view the Shenandoah Valley and Alleghenies.

The next year Lederer tried twice to penetrate the Blue Ridge, and failed. But in 1671, an expedition left Fort Henry (the frontier trading post that became Petersburg) and marched west. Striking the Staunton River, they reached the site of present Roanoke — thus penetrating the Blue Ridge—in less than two weeks. Accompanied by friendly Indians they pushed on to today's Radford. Reaching the beautiful New River Valley, across the Allegheny Divide, they found someone had been there ahead of them: three miles past the great watershed, they saw the inexplicable letters M A. N I. carved on a tree, plus "several other scratchments."

Dr. Lederer and the men of the Fort Henry expedition — Thomas Batts, Thomas Wood, Robert Fallam, John Weason, and an Appomattox Indian chief, Perecute—have been strangely neglected in Virginia's pantheon. But their adventures early in the reign of King Charles II were far braver, and more signifi cant, than the well-publicized junket nearly half-a-century later by Governor Alexander Spotswood, in whose heart throbbed the instincts of a public relations man and benign land promoter. It was Spotswood's tour that caught the public fancy, although hunters had proved for years that the Shenandoah— the Valley of Virginia — was little more dangerous than the settled east. The Valley had a history of numerous Indian settlements, but they were deserted around the time of Jamestown's founding. It's possible the Iroquois, Senecas, Shawnees, and lesser-known Indians who traditionally controlled the Valley had agreed to make it neutral ground, a place for hunting and trade, eschewing permanent settlements.

Until well into the eighteenth century eastern Virginians remained sluggish about crossing the mountain. Spotswood, with about a dozen cronies of the Tidewater quality "well-guarded by Indian scouts and frontier rangers," led his bibulous tour group (a diarist recorded endless toasts from a huge traveling liquor supply) to the banks of the Shenandoah River. There they buried a bottle with a paper claiming the land for King George I, and knocked back another round.

Flushed with the glory of it all when he returned to the capital at Williamsburg, Spotswood had another inspiration. He founded the Order of the Knights of the Golden Horseshoe, and presented each of his traveling companions with a miniature horseshoe set with precious stones. The expedition was an absolute artistic success.

But still the time wasn't right, and it would be ten years before the curtain rose on great Valley settlements and migrations. In 1728, the first of a new series of Crown land grants opened up the Valley to speculators like Tidewater moguls Robert Carter and William Beverley, and, perhaps more significantly, to northerners like Jacob Stover of Pennsylvania and Benjamin Borden of New Jersey.

The honor of being the Valley's first settler was claimed by a German whose name, Adam Miller, still rings with a quintessential Shenandoah sound. An immigrant from the Palatinate who arrived at Lancaster, Pennsylvania, in 1724, Miller heard of the Spotswood expedition, doggedly looped through eastern Virginia, and retraced the Golden Horseshoe route through Swift Run Gap, choosing his future homesite along the Shenandoah River near Massanutten Mountain. He returned to Pennsylvania for his wife and some friends, and around 1727, ahead of the grants, made the first known white settlement west of the Blue Ridge.

Other Germans came almost simultaneously, but unlike Miller of the long and hard way, they drifted down the linking valleys from Pennsylvania. Jacob Stover, a Swiss, was vastly energetic in obtaining grants and bringing in the German settlers whose descendants retain their ethnic stamp today. Yet Stover was close to the English authorities who controlled the grants and was related by marriage to Anglo pioneers: his father-in-law was the grandfather of Daniel Boone.

North of Staunton, around Harrisonburg and on to Winchester, lies Germanic Virginia. Those in doubt need only read the names on the mailboxes. Staunton itself was almost pure Scotch-Irish, as was the Valley from Staunton south. Unlike the stolid German farmers who, astride their own fertile limestone acres, rarely sought to stir again, the Scotch-Irish tended to roam farther, settle higher and wilder ground, and then, like as not, move on.

Thomas Walker and James Patton ranked high in the mid-eighteenth century settlement of the Shenandoah, but the man whose name lingered is John Lewis. He bought his land from the great William Beverley, a Tidewater Virginian, who built Beverley Manor on his mid-Valley project of 118,491 acres. Some of the building's walls are incorporated in today's Staunton Library. But it was Lewis who really founded Staunton. A brilliant leader, he, like other Ulstermen, was driven from northern Ireland by various forms of religious, economic, and political persecution. Lewis's tombstone still stands in the limestone-rich hills outside his old town. The epitaph says he "slew the Irish lord, settled Augusta County, located the town of Staunton and furnished five sons to fight the battles of the American Revolution." *He slew the Irish lord.* That's why he came: immigrants rarely spring from the safe and prosperous.

Staunton and Winchester were important centers in those vexing difficulties with the French and Indians that would occur at mid-century far away in the Ohio Valley tributaries. Young George Washington and Andrew Lewis (son of John) would earn their first battle stars during this time. Beyond the relative safety of Virginia eas of the Blue Ridge, eyes looked warily west to the fearsome Shawnee, across the dark Alleghenies.

To this day there remains an elusive core of mystery about the Shenandoah Valley, beginning with the Indian name which we cannot define. Some white settlers translated it as "sprucy stream;" others said, "place of the hills." The version that stuck, but may be too sweet for truth, is "daughter of the stars."

There is something, too, about the memory of all those restless multitudes: the vanishing Indians, the first blundering expeditions from the east, the trickle down from Pennsylvania,

Living history demonstrations at Fredericksburg echo the town's Civil War calamities.

the torrent that jammed the Valley Pike and Midland Trail. All the Indian fighters, the debonair gentlemen-explorers, the farmers, the teamsters, the drovers, the soldiers, the shaggy hunters with long rifles. All of them moving. The valley came to symbolize not only a destination of storied beauty, but something to remember on the road to somewhere else. *Oh Shenandoah* was the song of a man a thousand miles from oceans, beside the wide Missouri, thinking of a better-loved Virginia river. But the song is a sea chanty. Does that tell us something? Were these worn and nearly endless Southern mountains like the waves of a cosmic ocean, too vast for sound or foam?

Bearing little likeness to the plantation-rooted culture of the east, the Valley demanded small towns. The Scotch-Irish had a particular gift for handy, appealing communities. Of all the towns they sprinkled across the Shenandoah and surrounding mountains, Lexington was perhaps their masterpiece. The builders of old Lexington took the day's prevailing architecture (federal and Greek revival) and reworked it to a pure simplicity, a grace of proportion, that reflected the purpose of their lives. The best example is the Washington College group on the Washington and Lee University campus, which combines strength, scale, and serenity to perfection.

Not everybody agreed, especially strangers from eastern Virginia who came to enroll in W&L or at the adjoining campus of Virginia Military Institute. One such nineteenth century youth would recall, "I had heard of their race, and heard them described, long before I went there; and now I was among them, — those old McDowells, and McLaughlins, and McClungs, and Jacksons, and Paxtons...all the tribe of Presbyterians of the Valley...a type of humanity wholly new to me."

"Their impress was upon everything in the place. The blue limestone streets looked hard. The red brick houses, with severe stone trimmings and plain white pillars and finishings, were stiff and formal. The grim portals of the Presbyterian church looked cold as a dog's nose. The cedar hedges in the yards, trimmed hard and close along straight brick pathways, were as unsentimental as mathematics."

But I ask you, what do flatlanders know?

Nature bequeathed to Lexington the finest setting of any Virginia city. The Valley is narrow, with Blue Ridge and Allegheny ranges close in. Just outside town stands Lexington's Fujiyama, House Mountain. Lucky the town with its own geologic trademark. Lucky the people who can look to House Mountain in a spring twilight, when a great black roiling cloud splits over the summit and etches the sky with gray veils of rain, a scene from a Victorian lithograph. There is no gentle, peaceful rain here. It comes in roaring sheets, heralded in thunderclaps like VMI cannon.

VMI is part of the reason Lexington is the Valhalla of the Confederacy. Thomas J. Jackson, an obscure antebellum professor here, quickly became immortal as the military genius we call Stonewall. Most of his troops were Valley men comprising the ferocious Stonewall Brigade, and VMI provided many officers for the cause. When Jackson was killed, he was carried to Lexington for burial, in the graveyard on South Main. Today the only house he ever owned, brought back to its severe 1850s authenticity, is part of Lexington's memorable downtown restoration.

* * *

In 1865, Robert E. Lee accepted the presidency of almost-defunct Washington College, and for five years he not only rebuilt the school (renamed at his death to add his name), but provided unswerving moral leadership for the defeated South. When he died, his office was left untouched, and thus it has remained for 110 years. They buried him nearby in the campus chapel crypt.

Now let us look for a moment at his recumbent statue, in front of the chapel under the battle flags, at the Valhalla of the Confederacy. It will be hard for a non-Southerner to understand this. For that matter, any Southerner below the age of fifty will have a different outlook. So will all the South's future generations. But Virginians my age touched the last raveled battle streamer of the Stars and Bars. We remember the Confederates.

I had slight speaking acquaintance with two. They were scrawny-necked, confused, gentle old men of impossible age. One of them had served in Lee's Army of Northern Virginia for almost four years. Their last national encampment was in Norfolk, around

1949. By the late 1950s all of them were gone. The years of reunions and parades were over. The medals were put away.

The aura that surrounded those old rebels is what I would convey. It was something implicit: they simply had this fate-haunted quality, because they had done what they had done. The honor freighted upon them was absolute. Our deference was automatic. It was summatory. It was incontestable. Confederate veterans were, *ipso facto*, heroes. Nothing else they did with their lives, range as they might from utter probity to rakehell failure, could alter by one jot the esteem and affection that flowed from generations of Southerners. I guess the fact that they lost — lost with Uncle Robert, our tribe's perfect, gentle knight, lying up there in cold marble like some medieval figure — accounted for some of the emotional bite. I've asked Northerners about it, and I'm sure their attitude toward the Grand Army of the Republic was not the same. The Yankees felt honor, respect, friendly gratitude for their old soldiers. But our feeling was seasoned in tragedy. It was failure and subjugation in the common past which stamped the Lost Cause with such ineffable melancholy, and gave us such trenchant perception.

Our soldiers really were something. "They were the dirtiest men I ever saw, a most ragged, lean, and hungry set of wolves. Yet there was a dash about them that the Northern men lacked. They rode like circus riders. Many of them were from the far South and spoke a dialect I could scarcely understand. They were profane beyond belief and talked inces-

Living jewels beside a mountain stream, butterflies brighten the Allegheny Mountains.

santly." So said a Marylander who watched the Rebel army on its way to Sharpsburg.

Hungry, shoeless, often outmanned two to one, finally five to one, they held off the tide for four years. Is that how heroes are made? In the final analysis, the real granite in the relationship may have been this: putting aside all the esoterica of causes and issues, they were defending their homes.

For generations the reminders were everywhere. Virginia's roadsides were thickets of gaunt, silver-painted cast iron historical markers. No motor trip could avoid the terse chapter-by-chapter labeling of our mutual disaster. *Where Ashby Fell. The Seven Days. Early's Last Battle. The Death of Jackson. Mosby's Midnight Raid. Grant's Operations. Eve of Appomattox. Lee's Last Camp.* I think there's been a gradual erosion of the markers in recent decades, through vandalism and economies, and of course they're not on the Interstates, where most drive now.

Just over twenty years ago, when construction on the Interstate system reached its peak, I bought an electronic metal locator and joined the secretive fraternity of relic hunters. It was, and is, a pursuit tarnished by a certain percentage of trespassers and despoilers of designated battlefield parks and shrines. But where bulldozers were snorting through rights-of-way, splintering oaks, sweet gums, and pines, and biting into the trenches that still encircled our cities, there was an incomparable chance to gather relics that otherwise would lie under tons of concrete and blacktop. Even skilled battlefield pickers were startled by the quantity of metal in the ground: the buckles and insignia, the muskets and cannon balls, the still-cocked Colts and Remingtons and the bullet-punctured canteens. In a corner of the battlefield where The Seven Days began, I found what was, by all the evidence, the site of a small field hospital for McClellan's Union Army. Among the ground's silent witnesses was a .58 caliber musket bullet, strangely deformed. It resembled a wad of discarded chewing gum. When I showed the lead lump to a dentist, he said, yes, those are human tooth marks.

Today, most of the big battlefields are at least partially preserved in national and state parks. In museums and visitor centers the latest audio-visual techniques explain what happened. I'm sure any reincarnated veteran of 1861-65 would be bewildered. He might ask why we keep stirring the ashes.

When the battle of Fredericksburg was at its peak, as Pelham's artillery and Jackson's infantry crushed Burnside in a textbook demonstration of military éclat, Lee listened as the bloodcurdling Rebel yell came quavering from the front. The commander, eyes flashing, turned to Longstreet and said, "It is well that war is so terrible. We should grow too fond of it."

In Lexington, Lee the rebuilder told his people to abjure the might-have-beens, to let the past be the past, to get on with life. Virginians tried, and partially succeeded. But even now, no matter how deeply buried by the march of years, there is a faint, unrepentant, ineradicable refrain in the Virginia psyche. It says, *Look away, Dixie Land.*

* * *

Somewhere between Lexington and Roanoke, the Shenandoah Valley ends and Southwest Virginia begins. Before we go that far, we must take an overview from that 106-mile highway in the sky, the Skyline Drive, and its 215-mile continuation, the Blue Ridge Parkway. (Actually, the Parkway goes on much farther, through North Carolina to Great Smokies National Park.)

Thus, 321 miles of mountaintop road overlooks Virginia, much of it in Shenandoah National Park. Sometimes the view is toward the Valley, sometimes the Piedmont. All of it is beautiful. There are hundreds of stops and overlooks for the lazy and car-bound, but to appreciate the mountain with any intimacy requires some unhurried time, and some effort. Then you will be rewarded by glimpsing a family of waddling bears, grazing deer, the pale jewel of a wild orchid. Take one of the dozens of hiking trails, like the hemlock-festooned path to Dark Hollow Falls. A perfect name for that enchanted spot, Dark Hollow Falls suggests buckskin-clad hunters stopping to refresh themselves, or young lovers, members of feuding clans, slipping off to grapple on mossy banks.

Overnight accommodations along the way are placed scenically, so that your lodge room deck hangs on the edge of a cliff facing across the Valley to the purple Alleghenies, where sunsets flare like coals. The clouds themselves come churning past your door; you're at the 4,000-foot elevation, on the cliffs called Stony Man. Climb a few hundred feet more to the very summit, and you may be rewarded by the take off of a raven, soaring out for some lazy spins in space.

Virginians love driving on their mountains, and their favorite time is certainly fall. It's hard to predict the color change precisely, but usually in late September the dogwood and black gum flash red to alert us the show is beginning; then poplar, buckeye, and beech follow in early October with warm yellows. Red and yellow maples and dark purple oaks round out the mid-to-late October colors.

On the Valley side, where the pioneer Germans settled, lies Virginia's cave country. The entire Valley, vast bed of dolomitic limestone that it is, is undershot with caves, and several major examples have attracted visitors for more than a century. Curiously, our caves are popular spots for weddings. The decorations are permanent, created drop by drop through the rolling milennia by some careless, cosmic sculptor. There are pure white, crystal flowers, stalactites and stalagmites in the shape of domes, curtains, columns, even fried eggs. There are unseen residents, as well. A little beetle, born without eyes, joins a blind snail, and all-white crayfish, shrimp, and salamanders in the caves' bizarre menagerie.

The Skyline Drive/Blue Ridge Parkway is roughly paralleled for most of its northeast-to-southwest gradient through Virginia by the Appalachian Trail. Allied with Shenandoah National Park, with all its facilities — visitor centers, trails, programs, campgrounds, lodges — there's probably nothing comparable for conveniently enjoying and studying nature. But for those demanding sterner tests, George Washington and Thomas Jefferson National Forests, west of the Blue Ridge, in the Alleghenies, contain 1.5 million acres of public land, a wilderness covering much of western Virginia.

Roanoke, our major city west of the Blue Ridge, is gateway to southwest Virginia. Though a settlement was made there in the mid-eighteenth century, nearby Salem enjoyed greater success. Perhaps Roanoke's original name had something to do with its sluggish development. For most of its life the town styled itself Big Lick. About a century ago, the new Norfolk and Western Railway

Commercial daffodil farming in Gloucester County aims at northern markets.

established a major terminal there, and the place celebrated its fortune by adopting a more euphonious handle. Thereafter, it grew rapidly.

Richmonders, especially the bureaucrats who run Virginia's government, are sometimes wrongly accused of thinking the state ends at Roanoke. It's our loss if we do, for the country beyond is beautiful and there lingers a strong trace of pioneer days. Southwest Virginia resembles an Indian spear point, aiming straight for Cumberland Gap. Here ran the Warriors' Path, where Boone and his rifle-toting followers went west. Virginia's highest peaks, 5,729-foot-high Mount Rogers, and 5,520-foot White Top, dominate a vast outdoor complex formed by the union of Mount Rogers National Recreation Area and Virginia's Grayson Highlands State Park.

The towns vary west of Roanoke, depending on whether you're in coal or non-coal country. Giant Virginia Tech, the state's preeminent university for agricultural and engineering pursuits, dominates Blacksburg. Abingdon, like Lexington, recalls early nineteenth century Scotch-Irish Virginia. It's also home to one of America's most appealing theater institutions, the Barter Theater, founded at the pit of the Great Depression by hungry Broadway actors who were happy to play for food. Around Abingdon and through much of the central southwest lies a pastoral land where fat cattle grace giddily swooping hills, lush with limestone and bluegrass. But west of the Clinch River begins the tumbled, rugged region called Appalachian plateau by geologists, and coal country by the rest.

See it. Don't be put off by dismal tales of Appalachia. There are places where empty plastic bleach bottles still pile in drifts along the creek banks, beside tipped-over hulks of cars. Miners are rarely impressed by a need for tidiness. But there is a fascination in the mine fields, a drama set against the harsh backdrop of coal tipples and clanking trains.

For the few outsiders who ever see the inside of a coal mine, it is the experience of a lifetime. Once I donned coveralls, hard hat, and lamp, and took a mine elevator down more than 1,300 feet. Then, slumped back in a mine car, we rumbled horizontally for two miles. At the working face, a forest of hydraulic jacks held the five-foot stone ceiling in place long enough for the men to remove

the coal and move on. The noise was intense, but when power shut off on the mechanical digging equipment, there came a profound silence. Then I heard a series of unearthly musical booms and clangs.

"What's that?" I asked the shadow beside me, hunched over, like me, amid the jacks.

"Roof's working," he said, and spat.

I accepted a chew of Red Man as he explained that the rocks were moving around above us.

One of the surprises in a mine is the wind. It's artificial, of course, pumped in by giant fans. The silent, strong gale never ends, and in the beam of your helmet light, coal dust churns and sparkles like diamond dust.

I've always found miners friendly and colorful people who like to talk. And the way they talk out here, in which right is *raht*, like is *lahk*, is unlike speech anywhere else in Virginia. I am glad that coal is making a comeback, and that the inexhaustible supply of Virginia bituminous now rumbles toward far-off Hampton Roads (and the stacked-up colliers) in lengthening trainloads. I hope it brings new prosperity along the coal creeks to big company miners and "dog hole" diggers alike. Mining coal is dirty, dangerous, and strangely seductive. Miners rarely want to do anything else. In the language of the hills, *I hope them luck*.

Coal country holds one of the earth's strangest natural phenomena, Natural Tunnel. A cavern 850 feet long, as tall as a ten-story building, this monstrous hole in the mountains was carved by a very determined stream. A railroad runs through Natural Tunnel, which is open to visitors hiking Natural Tunnel State Park. The tunnel and its assorted cliffs and chasms reward the leg-cramping walks that must be taken for the best views. Another curiosity of the region, "The Breaks," is shared with Kentucky. Along that rugged border the Russell Fork River has carved the largest canyon in eastern America 1,600 feet deep and five miles long.

And finally we reach Cumberland Gap, on the borders of Kentucky and Tennessee. Here is the notch in the mountains where Boone showed the way west. We have come almost five hundred miles from Virginia's Atlantic beaches. We are farther west than Detroit. Montgomery, Alabama, and Columbus, Ohio are closer to us here than Richmond.

Virginia's capitol. Designed by Jefferson, it is one of America's supreme architectural treasures.

Chicago, and St. Louis are no farther away than Norfolk from Cumberland Gap.

Having come all this way, I see I have made some signal omissions. Some of them I'm not too worried about. Population trends, industrial development, the total cigaret production last year, the amount of zinc ore mined, and the situation vis-a-vis ground water and solid waste.

It would be pleasing to point out an assembly of current Virginia statesmen on whose shoulders the mantle of Thomas Jefferson would gracefully fit. Our state government is careful, clean, and — as governments go — capable. If it is not also creative, then perhaps it is as Voltaire said: "There is little charm, for active minds, in standing for tradition and authority." The percentage of lawyers in Virginia's General Assembly is one of the nation's highest. It makes us wonder, had the Spanish settlement thrived, how different things might have been, for Madrid sent no lawyers to America, lest they should multiply disputes among the Indians.

Virginia is served by some excellent newspapers. One of them, the *Richmond News Leader*, has the supreme good fortune to be home base for the nation's top cartoonist, Jeff MacNelly. He has won two Pulitzer prizes for his mordacious political cartoons. And in his comic strip, *Shoe*, a cast of hilarious birds parodies middle class life for the entertainment of loyal subscribers of more than six hundred dailies.

But Virginia is in something of a literary lull. Not too long ago, Richmond gave shelter and inspiration to novelists Ellen Glasgow and James Branch Cabell, and that supreme biographer, Douglas Southall Freeman. John Dos Passos lived in Westmoreland County, near the Lees and Washingtons. Today? We can claim kinship with William Styron, Tom Wolfe, and Tom Robbins, but they moved away. We're about due for a literary revival.

The lively arts do well here. Richmond has a permanent symphony, and Norfolk an opera company. The Virginia Museum of Fine Arts maintains its own repertory theater, which with the Barter of Abingdon leads Virginia's professional stage. Norfolk, Hampton, Richmond, and Roanoke have big coliseums, which join northern Virgina's Wolf Trap Park in guaranteeing non-stop headline performances.

But having said all that, and come so far, the question remains: has Virginia produced a definable Virginia character? What is the sum, in accumulated personality, of those four hundred years since the Jesuits began their settlement?

Defining regional differences is a precarious game, but overall, Virginia is a place where manners and taste still count for a great deal. It is an outpost of gentility, though clearly a besieged one. At the risk of waxing sentimental about the past, it seems to me that the generation of my parents —the one that grew up in the first quarter of the twentieth century — had an edge. I refer to such qualities as honesty, trust, wit, balance. Playing by the rules. Personal responsibility.

Virginians, especially of that generation, tend to meet strangers with a sort of absent-minded grace, with eyes focused on some distant horizon. A stranger may wonder if he is being understood. The answer is yes, but he is probably not being taken too seriously. The Virginian, like the Oriental, has a firm sense of historical sweep, of destiny, of his place on the broad river of time.

Two major social syndromes mark our recreational habits. In eastern Virginia, we're always *Going to the River*. The expression baffles outsiders, even western Virginians, who ask, what river? What do you do there? It sounds possibly sinister. No, they are assured, *Going to the River* is how an eastern Virginian has fun. The river is unimportant (it can be the Potomac, York, James, Mattaponi, Rappahannock, or Pamunkey). What matters

is that he has, or rents, a cottage overlooking water. It can range from an eighteenth century manor down to a cinder block hovel reeking with mildew and buzzing with wasps. Activities include fishing (for blues and shad), boating, playing bridge, having a few belts, watching the Washington Redskins, and steaming crabs to death in a tin pot. Steamed crabs, aflame with red pepper, are the eastern Virginian's chief delicacy. Should any Virginian invite you to *The River*, do not go unless you enjoy doing, and eating, appropriately.

The western Virginia equivalent is *Going to Camp*. We do not mean by that packing into the wilderness with tent and Coleman stove. *Camp* is anything from a slab hut to a ten-room stone and log lodge, garnished with antlered heads and bearskin rugs, and in fact it is likely to be far more comfortable than *The River*, with pleasant smells like pine boards and hot bread. Activities include fishing (for trout, smallmouth bass, or redeye), hiking through the National Forest which is always near, canoeing if the stream (preferably the Calfpasture, Cowpasture, or Bullpasture) is big enough, shooting a .22 up against the side of a ridge, playing bridge, having a few belts, and watching the Washington Redskins. There is no western equivalent for steamed crabs, although buckwheat cakes and sausage, with Highland County maple syrup, come close.

East or west, Virginians agree that aged ham is near the top of their all-time favorite food list, but they fall out immediately over whether it should be Smithfield or Country. Too oily, too salty, too hard, too loose, are typical charges hurled by ham votaries. In other delicacies, each side of the Blue Ridge has a monopoly on at least one superb asset: peanuts (water-blanched, please) from the south, maple syrup and sugar from the northwest, are eagerly sought.

A culture reveals something with its food and drink. Only in recent years (coinciding with the legalization of liquor-by-the-drink) has there been a revival of the tradition of public conviviality that once marked Virginia's taverns. And nowhere has tavern society enjoyed such a rebirth as in Richmond, where less than twenty years ago it was an article of faith that nobody went out. These days, Virginians of all ages and races gather

in the capital's Shockoe Slip establishments.

I was in one such restaurant, near the table where half–a–dozen elderly West End matrons were having lunch in a pleasant, blue-haired circle. When it was time to go, they began the pushing back, the scraping and groaning, and rising, that was plainly hard for some of them. Amid that careful tottering, one woman shot briskly to her feet and strode off, leading the way. But another, slower woman called her back and delivered a short lecture.

"Don't *ever* let me see you jump up like that and run off," she said. "It's dangerous. What you must do, don't you know, is rise slowly and then stabilize yo'self."

In all, it was not a bad epigram, a summary of how Virginians view their four-century-old game. *Rise slowly and stabilize yourself.*

And then move ahead.

Southside Virginia, along the North Carolina border, is a conservative region where old ways cling tenaciously. Even so, the glimpse of a patient mule is a rare sight today.

Richmond, Virginia's capital and financial center, began as a trading post in the 1600s at the upper navigable limit of the James River. Here is the site today, looking from the south bank to the city's heart, with the new Federal Reserve Bank building at left center. *Right:* Spring festival concert on Richmond's Monument Avenue.

The Shenandoah Valley, an irregular basin extending some one hundred and seventy-five miles from Roanoke to Winchester, received its fertility from underlying limestone, its ethnic cast from Scotch-Irish and German settlers. Here, Stonewall Jackson's "foot cavalry" achieved military fame. *Left:* Virginia winter, just severe enough to be scenic, grips Goochland County.

The coastal waters' renewable bounty brings more than $60 million annually to Virginia watermen like these crabbers. *Right:* Sometimes more swamp than river, the Chickahominy still supports remnants of Virginia's Indian tribes. *Overleaf:* Chesapeake Bay crab pounds, locked in the ice of an uncommonly hard winter.

Small oyster dredge boats brave the winter swells for bivalves from Bay and Atlantic alike. Connoisseurs distinguish origin by saltiness and color. Natives term the process "drudging." *Left:* A retired waterman, home from the sea. *Overleaf:* Norfolk's Gardens-by-the-Sea blaze with azaleas, camellias, myriad other blooms.

The U.S. National Park Service preserves the historic scenery of Cumberland Gap, where a western sun like this one beckoned Daniel Boone and his pioneer bands. *Right:* South Fork of the Tye River, down the east side of the Blue Ridge, is a favorite retreat in Nelson County.

Mount Rogers, at 5,729 feet Virginia's highest point, dominates a rugged recreation zone that sprawls across five counties in Southwest Virginia. Trailside splendors like this mossy grove grace the great mountain's flank. *Left:* Cypress knees rise from the dark, notably pure swamp waters of Seashore State Park, Virginia Beach.

With a metropolitan population greater than 600,000, Richmond supports a vigorous cultural agenda, including the popular Richmond Ballet. *Right:* With hisses, gulps, and clouds of acrid smoke, a crucible of molten brass is skillfully poured into iron-bound molds of sand by the Colonial Williamsburg foundryman.

Early settlers found much to amaze them, yet a familiar flora made an Englishman feel almost at home. *Left:* Their work done, homely milkweed pods wait the cold of an Appalachian winter, normally severe for only two months.

The dogwood blossom, Virginia's state flower, is the perfect excuse for a plethora of local springtime festivals. *Right:* Monticello, a marvel of grace filled with ingenious concepts and devices, was Jefferson's home and center of his lifelong pursuit of science, political truth, beauty, and good living. *Overleaf:* A Nelson County stream.

Southern terminus of Virginia horse country, Albemarle County is a favorite of wealthy newcomers, many of them agitating to own fauna like this yearling thoroughbred. *Left:* Fog creeps over the Shenandoah Valley near Luray. *Overleaf:* Near Highland County's Hightown, are headwaters of the James and Potomac rivers.

Ready for a sports car rally or a football game, a Richmond Jaguar stares at the falling leaves. *Right:* Redbud trees welcome spring to the Blue Ridge Parkway, a highway in the sky featuring wayside overlooks, nature trails, and preserved mountain culture.

Virginia's longest, harshest winters are part of life in the high Alleghenies. On this farm near Monterey, sheep and split rail fences recall an earlier America. *Left:* Moonlight glows on snowy fields near Warrenton in Northern Virginia, land made famous by the raider John S. Mosby, the Confederacy's Gray Ghost.

On other statues Virginians carved complete names and dates, but when they raised this mighty equestrian statue in Richmond to their Confederate chieftain, they inscribed just one word: LEE.

On tiny Tangier Island, a precariously placed speck of land in the center of Chesapeake Bay whose entire economy is based on the water; boats—not cars—occupy the residential parking places.

Aground in Chesapeake Bay, a derelict trawler becomes a piece of Homeric playground equipment for the venturous youth of Tangier Island. *Left:* Birds by the millions visit or dwell on Virginia's Barrier Islands. They include ten species of hawks (the endangered peregrine falcon is one), whistling swans, and Forester's tern.

Chincoteague's ocean trawler fleet helps give Virginia fourth rank among U.S. seafood producers. *Left:* Only electric motors are permitted on Diascund Reservoir near Newport News, where this early-morning fisherman trolls for lunker bass. *Overleaf:* Lemminglike start of the Richmond marathon.

Across Virginia, maples like these Richmond specimens blare brassy greetings to autumn. *Left:* The siren beauty of Crabtree Falls lures hikers to the eastern slope of the Blue Ridge. *Overleaf:* A merchant ship glides under a storm in Norfolk's harbor.

Near Monterey, in the heart of the Alleghenies, vistas are stunning but job opportunities few; hence, the population of Virginia's remotest corner has declined through the twentieth century. *Right:* Veteran Blue Ridge hikers savor fleeting instants of transient beauty, like this maple leaf in a glass-clear stream.

Norfolk's Willoughby Spit is a relaxed neighborhood anchoring the south end of the world's greatest harbor, Hampton Roads. Causeway on the horizon is part of the bridge-tunnel crossing the harbor's mouth. *Left:* Shells at Chincoteague manifest richness of the nearby waters, where Tom's Cove may produce the finest oysters.

The Elizabeth River, an arm of the port of Norfolk, separates the big port city from Portsmouth, its neighbor on the opposite bank. With Newport News and Hampton across Hampton Roads, the four comprise tidewater's mightiest port complex.

Far from the sea, the Shenandoah Valley developed along different cultural lines. Scotch-Irish settlers established a fiercely independent tradition combined with a reverence for learning and built farms and schools among the rolling hills.

At Williamsburg (the Old Capital, as it's sometimes called) stand almost ninety original buildings, and reconstructions bring the total to some five hundred. Here, mile-long Duke of Gloucester Street is captured late on an autumn afternoon. *Right:* In Williamsburg's foundry, a lit candlestick illuminates molds.

A Gloucester County beekeeper waits for results from his latest outdoor advertising campaign. *Left:* The busy pacing of a Shetland pony tracks a winter landscape near Warrenton in Fauquier County. *Overleaf:* Like cotton candy, fog rolls through Cumberland Gap, Virginia's westernmost extremity, five hundred miles from sea.

Hanover County, home of Patrick Henry, retains a rural flavor despite incursions by metropolitan Richmond. *Left:* On the Blue Ridge Parkway stands historic Mabrey's Mill, Virginia's nomination for the world's most picturesque water mill. *Overleaf:* From Arlington, where the Marine Corps Monument recalls Iwo Jima, the nation's capital lies just across the Potomac River.

Always bent on recovering ground, the forest closes on an old mill near Cumberland Gap. *Right:* More than 60 percent of the Civil War was fought on Virginia soil. In Fredericksburg, "living history" demonstrates the way it was.

Virginia's children: A game of football enlivens the sober panorama of downtown Richmond. *Left:* Just upstream from the capital, in Goochland County, a modern Tom Sawyer heads for a spring day's fishing in the James, the most quintessentially Virginian river. It traverses the state from mountains to sea.

In the Alleghenies, only river-bottom land encourages farming. This abandoned rake once toiled beside an exceptionally scenic tributary of the James called the Cowpasture, a favorite recreation site in northwest Virginia.

Split rail fences survive in a few rare settings, thanks to iron-hard locust rails, and a few tradition-minded folk who keep the structures repaired. This example endures near the ski resort of Wintergreen.

Circe of the forest, a young rider in central Virginia woods may unknowingly retrace tracks of the Knights of the Golden Horseshoe, Redcoat General Banastre Tarleton, or Jeb Stuart's cavalry. *Right:* Far to the west, in Cumberland Gap, this ancient road recalls the feet of Shawnees, early pioneers, and settlers' wagons.

Fine horseflesh and the elegantly earthy culture of the hunt: against the backdrop of Carter Hall in Clarke County, the Blue Ridge Hunt sets forth behind the master of foxhounds. *Left:* Equines of another stripe—wild ponies of uncertain origin—enjoy life more informally on Assateague Island, northernmost of Virginia's barriers. *Over-leaf:* Wintering geese at Back Bay, Virginia Beach.

Traditional family farms — though few are as traditional as this one in Madison County — still dominate Virginia agriculture. Many who settled here in the Blue Ridge foothills were displaced by the formation of Shenandoah National Park fifty years ago. *Left:* Performer waits his turn at Galax Old Fiddlers' Convention. *Overleaf:* Thoroughbred only in charm — the Assateague pony.

Within the commuting orbit of Washington, D.C., the idyllic horse country around Middleburg equals some of Virginia's most expensive real estate. *Right:* Even in winter, Virginia Beach retains devotees.

Norfolk's revived downtown surprises returning Navy veterans who remember the bad old days of World War II. The round building is Scope, the city's entertainment and convention center. *Left:* Another nuclear submarine goes down the ways at Newport News Shipbuilding and Dry Dock Company, a leading American shipyard since the nineteenth century.

Privates, generals, and unknowns: the veterans of many wars find peace, "On Fame's eternal camping ground," Arlington National Cemetery. *Right:* In this peaceful setting at the village of Appomattox Court House, the Civil War ended with the historic meeting of Generals R. E. Lee and U. S. Grant.

Despite storms and occasionally capricious shorelines, tidewater Virginians and their houses cling to precious beaches. *Left:* Old Cape Henry Light, on right, built in 1791, was authorized by the nation's first congress. "New" Cape Henry Light is now a century old. They have witnessed such nautical dramas as the sinking of German U-boats. Today, they overlook lines of giant, waiting coal ships.

Famed oceanographer Matthew Fontaine Maury thought Goshen Pass, near Lexington in the Alleghenies, one of earth's most beautiful spots. He directed that his funeral cortege pass by here. The river was then renamed the Maury. *Right:* In Henrico County, winter's icy pendulum counts the hours. *Overleaf:* Fish traps at the Eastern Shore's Cape Charles testify to the sea's ageless fecundity.

Getting the job done on a Piedmont farm. *Left:* Hundreds of miles of trails, including the Maine-to-Georgia Appalachian Trail, wind through Shenandoah National Park. *Overleaf:* Fall foliage attracts visitors to isolated Highland County. In early spring, they return to buy locally produced maple syrup.

Abrams Falls in far-west Washington County is one of Virginia's lesser-known scenic exemplars. *Right:* Along the Blue Ridge Parkway, a snail contemplates a beautiful rhododendron blossom as spring reaches the mountains.